CATHERINE CARSON

THE
Land Of

OPPOSITE ATTRACTIONS

BELLE ISLE BOOKS
www.belleislebooks.com

Copyright © 2022 by Catherine Carson

No part of this book may be reproduced in any form or by any electronic or mechanical means, or the facilitation thereof, including information storage and retrieval systems, without permission in writing from the publisher, except in the case of brief quotations published in articles and reviews. Any educational institution wishing to photocopy part or all of the work for classroom use, or individual researchers who would like to obtain permission to reprint the work for educational purposes, should contact the publisher

ISBN: 978-1-953021-65-6
LCCN: 2022901064

Cover designed by Chelsea Glowacki
Project managed by Haley Simpkiss

Printed in the United States of America

Published by
Belle Isle Books (an imprint of Brandylane Publishers, Inc.)
5 S. 1st Street
Richmond, Virginia 23219

BELLE ISLE BOOKS
www.belleislebooks.com

belleislebooks.com | brandylanepublishers.com

To Mom, Dad, Nicole, and Connor:
I could not have done this without you.
Thank you for all the years and all the material—
I love you more than words (and that's saying something).

THE
OTHER

Blooms

Cream petals stuck to the steps
in the same way that
melted ice cream slides down
a spoon.

Soft, the color of
warm bones. I couldn't stop
thinking about the contagion of
color.

Those soul-sucking
blooms.

Koi

You float around like a fish in my head.
Lily pads bob at the surface; you swim
underneath. I am the water.

What must you think when you watch
the light pour in, shaky pillars
of clarity illuminating the murk?

Or do you swim, fat-bodied and sleek,
off to some other great pond,
headed for cleaner waters?

That's Love

After sex the other night,
you realized pasta dough was stuck
to your fingernails.

It took us an hour and a half to
make fettuccine and twenty minutes
to make love.
I wish it were the other way around.

Today I painted a silly little painting
that made no sense, and I thought of
that patch of hair on your neck that a
razor's never touched.

The Land of Opposite Attractions

We have all the windows open, and
a song we don't know plays wistfully
in the background.
New radio, you say.

You perch and
watch people on the sidewalk,
laughing, eating, walking.
I brush your head and it shines
as a single hair.

That little eye beats in my chest
and you mumble to yourself.
We talk of lunch.

Bug Jars

Summer heat descended slowly
as a hard, anxious slumber.
I only noticed when the mosquitos
began to suck blood like
seven-cent lemonade.
The season has a peculiar way of
forcing nostalgia in dusty places.
Like how the first comet you
saw, illuminated in a blackening sky,
flew over your old, brick house.
I can imagine your face, full of
boyish wonder, staring at the glow.

The Land of Opposite Attractions

How, on that very street, you rode your
first bike, propelled not by fear or chance
but by your father's hands on the
small of your back. How the street swelled
with debris and branches after the hurricane.
Perhaps it is easier to recall someone else's
memories as your own.
I collect yours like bugs in a jar,
holes at the top so they
can breathe and live; so I can study them,
nurture them, then release.

Plant Me in the Solid Ground

Plant me in the solid ground
atop fertile life already in bloom.
Pluck me and twirl like a child caught in the
first rainstorms of the warmer months, and
watch as I spread out over the newly born
Earth.

Collect stamps from postcards my
breath sends to you. Save tears in ornamented
glass jars to count during our happier hours.
Etch my features into skin with your
callused fingertips.

The Land of Opposite Attractions

Hold me like the moon holds
a fresh day before she disappears into
the velvet night.

I listen to the sound of moving water
inside your voice; how streams gurgle
at the soft consonants of my name; how
light pricks the blue in your eyes
when you speak.

Plant me in the solid ground,
I say.

A Morning

I dream of a white kitchen.
A ceramic mug sits on the counter,
coffee staining a streak into its glassy side,
creamer running down the edge;
a hand reaches,
        grips firmly,
sips.

The morning
        is quiet in her
                arrival.

Outside, the world is waking too.
Dew slides down blades of grass and
caresses stems

       slowly in

              slumber.

Silently, your fingers slide
down my arms; I hadn't
       realized you were
here.

The morning is complete.
The conversations that piece together
a day begin, and privately I
wish for an
eternity.

Tragedy

A hurricane ravages a shore,
and people—an old woman,
a boy with skinned knees, a
mother-to-be—
are swept away.

Dust settles on bodies,
cradles soft bone,
steady into velvet night.

But couples, young and in love,
(the kind who memorize the creases of
each other's eyelids) get married with an
ocean background—

      a hazy sheet of glass
reflecting sky.

Why

      do my dreams come
coded in devastation,
drenched in joy,
dismantled into destiny?

A Passing

Blossoms, barely pink and held by the
shy weight of their own beauty,
tuck inward to brace against March's
winter whippings.

Why is Mother Nature under
such restraints—
that is, season?
Her strength measured only by the
thunder of her storms and not the
dropping of petals over a
spring dawn?

Can we not relive a summer moment
of irresponsible joy in the midst of
icy blue dreams?

Burst

The sky—pregnant with rain—lies heavy
as a thick quilt over the warm earth.
Lightning punctures
the beautiful tapestry like the
needles of God.

Whatever you are, I will become, too.
Here comes the omnipotent longing, holding
tightly to my beating animal heart as the
ceiling above me bursts into
vast precipitation.

Slowly, it cools the cement, and people
cautiously venture out again.
A sort of mist settles around shoulders
and ankles like a lost child clinging to me
in a way that says,
Take me home.

First Thing's First

First thing's first:
love is not a sunset.

I remember the wind blowing loose sand,
the water growing dark, dormant until
we saw it again.
Our watchtower sat among the reeds;
we climbed up together.
Little houses faded in the distance
like they were fighting sleep,
and the waves lapped like thirsty animals.
The last light blazed on over the water,
a flame melting into open ocean.

Love is not a sunset—it's the water that reflects it.
Love is not a sunset—the sun is too perfect.
We are the billions of sand particles, the dry reeds,
the desperate crashing of the waves.

First thing's first:
love is not a sunset; it's everything else.

Swallets

Like a swallet, our conversations sink down
beneath the floorboards of our first home,
making us lonely.
We tend to argue most when we agree.

If silence is the absence of narrative,
we wrote the fucking book.

Sometimes, like the thin lip of a wine glass
breaking against the counter,
desires shout their way into existence.
I am the glass—you are the broom.

A clash of symbols or the soft steps of
morning are memorialized by the
fluttering of eyelids.

I admit, my sensitivities are heaps of
kindling waiting for a flame, but I never asked
to be burned down.
Not tonight, anyway, when one less person
goes hungry and your mouth curls like the
first day we met.

Art Poem

She sipped tea—a note of honey—and
walked in silence through a hot room full
of hot bodies.

Small pearls of sweat formed shyly on
the nape of her neck, the canyon between
skin and hair.

The art stared back at her blankly.
How odd that she looks at each piece and sees
the same thing.

Black and white photos hung limp
against the wall, their color
faded and gone, like exhaustion.

People mused about, wandered with purpose,
but she stood still, her body swaying
in front of the photographs mindlessly.

You gently grabbed her elbow,
fingers long and kind like your body, and
led her home.

I Want a Girl

I want a girl with loose lips.
I want a girl who loves the smell of a Christmas
tree but kills it every year.
I want a girl who ignores the blisters on her feet;
who speaks too loudly in restaurants; who
never sleeps.
I want a girl as tough as a beer bottle
right before it breaks.
I want a girl who treats cat scratches and
heart attacks the same.
I want a girl who acts like a woman, who
knows gentleness is mandatory and breaks
dishes and lamps and elbows,
but never promises.
I want a girl who loves the slink of a cat but
hates the voices of people.
I want a girl to sweep into my life like the
shattering of glass and then fade like
hot breath on a window.

Sinful

Just flesh and juice;
sweetness, slightly
        overripe for your enjoyment.
Just pits and stems and seedy cores.

True, I am small—slightly bruised
from a fall down the muddy, time-worn
path made by eager children,

but my smooth skin (baking under sunlight)
still feels your calloused snatches.
Your greedy needs.

Why must I be picked, torn from
the boughs and the shade, for consumption?
Just for your appetite?

You: you are not gentle,
        with your nakedness,
your phallic nature.

What happened to the woman whose
skin was as soft as mine?
I am not the reason you sinned.

The Salamander

The sun permeated through the blank room
and
hurled itself against bare walls,
against white walls and white halls.

I've just come back from the river,
she said.
It was warm and I felt soft.

They laid out on rocks, she said.
They basked in the sun like lizards,
and I waited for my sun to come.

She held out her hand to catch a
salamander,
but it turned out to be a leach,
so she let it go.

The Accidental Baptism

We hiked through moss-covered forest,
trees standing like archaic pillars
holding up the dying sun.

The Blue Ridge lit up in front of us,
and its periwinkle haze receded from the
zenith. How grateful I was to be swaddled

in the divine.
The stream fought through solid
boulder to reach shade;
it spilled down into a cold pool.

We looked at each other, spoke the
language of I-dare-yous and knew
the moment before it was birthed.
Stripped of our clothes, we stood naked

like our first day, peering over the
edge. You waded in, soaking in the
mountain water cell by godly cell.
I have no patience for such—

I leapt.

The water took my body, a dying woman
between two hands, and revived me.
I lost gauge of temperature, as if
underneath the glass was a void.

My eyes fluttered open, just
for a moment,
and saw an emerald city.
I heard the waterfall above, now
just a shy gurgle, an afterthought of
the place beyond. The seconds froze like
crystals on a glass pane.

I emerged from the water in a single
shriek of bliss, a shock straight from the cannon.
The air sucked me into its vacuum, the waterfall
made a rushing sound, and voices called a name.

We stood there, naked and numb
among the elements. You, too, had seen it.
We walked westward,
toward that glowing, dying thing, and
drove home on wet towels.

VCR

The fire burning alongside the
shoulder of I-81 made me think of
our home movies.
Maybe it was the fuzz of the VCR
reflected off your wet face,
the color of smoke,
as we watched my sister and I
meet for the first time.

Nicole was so small, a tiny peapod covered
in dark hair; I was in love with her from the
very first day.
I sit in your lap, hold her
infant body in my arms—
we are stacked like the Russian dolls
you bought us some twelve years later.

The fire does not die, so someone (an older
man patting his bulging stomach)
pulls over to call a number.
I watch the smoke twist sleepily over

Afton mountain, wandering farther
away from home, and
drive north.

The Equalizer

Traces of her are all over our bodies—
cream-colored skin dusted with freckles,
ice-blue eyes like a hurricane,
a mole on a squared jaw.

We are her, but we do not know her.
How, widowed with a child, she held you
tightly and wept alone in a curtained room
while the phone rang and rang.

But now she sits, a living memorial for
all the years that have taken parts of her.

She buried her child with the same hands
that hold mine. Her voice shakes
over the phone, stutters and falls on words
that she once held as a lozenge on her tongue.

Perhaps when the world is asleep, when
darkness is the equalizer,
she dreams of them—the man she loved,
the man she didn't, her lost child,
you, me.

Tracing a Black Sky

You are the smell of raindrops kissing the earth—
pungent, dark, gentle.
You are every streak of lightning to ever
grace the untouched skies.
You are the look in someone's face when they
recognize a dear friend on a crowded bus.

I am not religious, but you make me wish
for a quiet salvation.
Our bodies are incomplete halves, but when
pieced together, they sing.
A warmth rises in my chest, and I know
you placed it there.

God, if there are
but so many days left under the sun, then let them
be filled with pockets of memories
containing you.

There is a cosmic shift over my head;
the constellations resemble your shining face.

Casual Ecstasy

You must be an electric boy.
You must be a boy who grew up hearing how
much he was loved.
Your mother must love you.

If I close my eyes and try hard enough,
I can feel the ridges in your fingertips
etch a map of veins over my skin.

I don't remember falling in love with you.
People don't notice their hair growing, or
the biting of fingernails, or the slow
rhythm of breath. You happened like a
quiet, biological phenomenon.

You are the simplest of moments compiled
into a mess of curls and ears and knees and
shoulders and eyelashes. You are every
freckle the sun puts on my body.
You are the scars on my stomach.
You are every tooth that has fallen out of my mouth
and all the times I've said your name aloud.

Every song I hear, I imagine how you would conduct it—
how you would wave your hands in the air
as if directing every sound.
Every constellation I see, I wonder if you
could tell me its name.

THE
SELF

Beautiful Things

Aging leaves take final leaps and
land softly on my windshield.
I study:

      veiny architecture, translucent skin like wet paper;

      like webs suspended in branches; like an eggshell
opening.

Something in me feels alive today; alive, aware, like I haven't been.

No hospitals, with their corrective smell and stained gowns; no silences;

no windowless rooms; no burning, throbbing guilt as I look at my mother.

Guilt throbbing like a toothache, I extract the rotten thing

slowly, painfully, then:

    freedom in blood.

My heart thumps evenly, ventricles thankful for relief.

My head is two pounds lighter.

My fingers find their way back to a pen, a semblance of

order, a life remembered.

But today,

    today there are just the leaves; translucent, beautiful
things.

Butterscotch

I want to write about the monarch's wing:

> how it splayed out next to the poor thing,
>
> ruined, crushed velvet on pavement.

I want to write about that morose feeling of

> wakeful slumber; sleepwalked into another room,
>
> turned right back around like a dream.

I want to write about the air this morning,

> cold as wet skin while we bustle about, hot
>
> blood churning in veins, hot breath everywhere.

How they make me grow quiet.

> How guilt forms like a cramp in my side.

But sometimes, even poets cannot feel with their

> whole selves. Love, sweet as butterscotch, turns
>
> bitter in our cold fingers.

Strangers remain strangers again.

Sentimentality

It rained just a few hours earlier.
The street pavement hissed; it spat
out steam, made the air damp.

A moving car is, by far, the
easiest place to practice the
habit of sentimentality,

propelling my
nightmares of loss. I cry
at the sight of roadkill.

Because what if that racoon
had a family? Was it a mother?
Enduring one more

fit of nostalgia makes
even the beautiful painful.
I long to look at the river and

see nothing but water.

Late Nights with Language

I want to have sex with you again.
Yes, the kind of love-making that
lingers
in my mind long after my body
is done.
I want to close my eyes and open my
mouth wide while you pull out
every word stuck in my throat.

More lustful than any mistress
twisted between a neighbor's sheets,
you sing down my spine and
settle
in me. Filled by you, conquered,
and yet the haze remains.
You are covered in mysteries my
eyes cannot see.

The Land of Opposite Attractions

I try and sound out your name,
give you a face, but you remain
invisible.
Wrap me up in arms like a house,
plant flowers along my edges,
paint me a new color, but please never

leave me in silence.

Land of the Midnight Sun
An ode to Nikki Giovanni's "Ego Tripping (there may be a reason why)"

I am never alone. Even standing here in the
land of the midnight sun, there is company.
Once I appreciate the silence, the moment of
choice suspended in warm air, the freedom of loud,
naked footsteps on a wooden floor; once I
acknowledge the beauty in this,
the melting begins—I thaw.

To know one's own strength is to value the
extraordinary—to bravely unleash a flood
upon the world. I am a powerful woman.
My grace lies in an unkempt ponytail,
my strength in the ache of an empathetic heart.
Women are like cigarettes: men prefer us
hanging from their mouths even while we burn,
our smoke filling the room;
like a glorious cancer, we spread.

The Land of Opposite Attractions

The curves of my hips outline a dreamy blue
mountain range; my tears turn to streams that
feed the Atlantic—I am the salt queen.
All the fish of the world swim in me.
When I speak, I pull the moon closer to listen,
and tides, a deep jade, turn under me.

No, I do not always feel my own force.
Some days it rains, and I lose myself in
earthly thoughts, a sub-lunar consciousness,
until my sisters from the land of the midnight sun
whisper to me—and I remember who I am.

Fruit Basket

The basket sits molding on the counter of
a shabby townhouse (leaking and fly-ridden),
but I ignore the rot. Riffling through it,
my hands touch bruised flesh and
pick through sticky stems.

I look down at my own body and
see hips sculpted by my mother's genes,
like the shape of a pear's bottom, the
golden-green skin stretching taut
over its mealy body. My breasts sag slightly
like overripe avocadoes, drooping at
the weight of areolas (the size of the pit)
cradled within the browning body.

The Land of Opposite Attractions

My stomach rolls over denim, soft
as a bruised banana, seeping through spotted peel.
Knees, too, the texture of kiwi skin—
covered in fuzz and smelling of earth.
The blueberries scattered along the bottom
of the basket (forgotten, purple)
resemble my eyes.

My hands reach down, split the peach
between my thighs until juice
(sweet and sticky and warm)
drips from golden flesh.

A Parallel Universe

In a parallel universe, maybe I would have been an astronaut.

Perhaps I would pull back my hair, yanking it quickly into a

ponytail, and pull my space helmet over it all.

Maybe I could have flown about up there, counted stars until

I understood them, surveyed planets for signs of life like ours—

cups of tea, rolled-up jeans wet from rain, joints of sativa.

Perhaps they would invite me to see their view:

Look over there, they'd say, and past all the darkness and

cosmos I would see home. A swirling little rock teeming with

everything I've ever known and loved.

The Land of Opposite Attractions

Stay for a while, they'd say. But could I leave?

Could I wake up foreign every morning?

No, I'd say. *Thank you, but I need to do a sink of dishes*

at home. And then I'd fly off, by myself, staring down the

cold abyss. I would float past all answers and all questions.

My body, soft and round, would be its own rocket ship.

Once home, I would finally wash my dishes and maybe

paint my toenails and close my eyes to see it all again.

I would paint everything behind my eyelids, behind the

veins, and leave no name.

The Deer

I had a dream the other night—
a deer with silver eyes, hit by a car.
Suddenly I was the driver,
my body curled over the deer's
body as if to protect it from death,
but it was already gone.

Those silver eyes, frozen wide open,
looking at something past me,
past the roads and damp forest and
animal pain.
It knew something I did not.

I keep quitting my jobs,
drinking cheap and anesthetizing liquor,
laughing when I don't mean it.
I'm tired of greasy tables, strangers
with loose dollars in their pockets,
the rattle of thoughts that eat like
mold, getting high by myself.

What did that deer know?

Two-Thirds

My first kiss was with the toilet bowl, a handsome
        prince of dirty water.
The sun set like a heavy heart in the sky,
        the suburban horizon catching its fall.

A dog barks somewhere in the distance, punctuating
        the air where it should lay silent.
I long to be in two-thirds:
        one-third body;
        one-third desperation;
an empty space to separate the two.

Things are going well; I can no longer sit in the
        bathtub, vertebrae smashed against linoleum
like the moon touches the blue mountain range,
        bursting at the peaks.

A small bird lands on a thin branch, its
        skeleton delicate as the veins of a leaf bending
in the late spring breeze.
        The breeze tastes like cotton candy.

I open my mouth to eat.

Bipolar

I.

The doctor adjusts his glasses;
tells me the news.
There isn't much else.
I leave the fluorescent hum of the
taupe-walled office
and beat my hands on the
steering wheel.
Failure has a funny taste,
like stale sunshine.
I feel my car take
a sharp turn.
A ringing in my ears tells me
I am not in another dream.
I get pink pills.

II.

Months later, I still feel as if
I swallowed a bellyful of moths.
Chronic, chronic, chronic rings
in my ears like a sick rhythm,
and I wonder if it will ever leave.
Sun touches my skin; I sit
like a cat in a window, basking.
I can still bask, I think.
A hurricane of guilt swells,
pushes against my sides,
refuses to be calmed.
People look at me strangely
afterward, but they don't know
I, too, tried to swim to the
eye.

Diagnosis

Under a gray sky, a fog enveloping
oblivion, rain blowing at unpleasant angles—
despair is welcome then; nurtured, even.

It's when the plants grow lush with
anticipation, grass regains its color, and
flowers burst through soil in their grand
declaration of life—
again and again, *life*—

that is when despair seems most bleak.

When the world opens itself up, and still
you are blind, despite yourself.

I Want to Be a Storm

Flashes of burnt anger, leaving a
pungent taste in the air; swirling with leaves
and thrashing with trees—making all the
booming sounds of the world.

I want to be a storm, to have permission
to hurl myself against the universe
and cry so hard I flood villages and
water flowers all at the same time.

I want people to fear me, to run
indoors and put their pets away, all
while the brave make forts and
confront what I can't.

Effortless

Words hang from me like dead flies on a strip
glued to an old ceiling fan.

They seep into my ears until all I can hear is a ringing,
and the only way to stop it is to eat them.

An idea is born like a child—painfully at first, but
you nurse them until they are just yours.

In bed, the words crawl under the sheets and cling to my
collarbones, where they nestle and spend the night
because they know I hate being alone.

During the day, they sit under my tongue, and I swallow
them when I get nervous.
I cheat; they always tell me what to say
so I don't have to think.

If I had to think, I would hate myself for never
becoming what I truly desired—
effortless.

The Widow

The five o'clock moon looked like a
stamp in need of ink, she said.
Blotted edges in need of color.

I think of her: the dunked witch; the
lousy harlot; the widowed woman.

How they laughed when she walked
head-down, when she couldn't write,
when she fasted on
the eleventh day of the moon.

She wore only white, the color of
mourning, her hair short and boyish as
she laid down her dying husband
among the Ganges' waters.

The eight o'clock moon looked
thumb-punched, she said.
A perfect hole in a thick sea of sky.

Baptism by Car Accident

Smoke from the hood suffocated me in that
shrinking box; then I was on knees, hands,
blindly searching for nothing among
shards of glass.
I wondered at first if I was dead.

I felt like the soggy apples beneath the trees
of the orchard, bruised and never picked.
My car looked like an aluminum can
crushed against a pole by some
invisible foot.

Sometimes a baptism takes place in
an ambulance.
The car is replaced, a hand is set wet,
in a cast, and everyone lives.

I am reminded of my life by the lump
on my left knee—a souvenir—
purple and sore when it rains.

Junk Drawer Poetry

I write because I have to;
choice flew out the window with the bat
stuck in the attic.

Poems fall like mealy fruit,
hanging heavy over the heads of schoolchildren
like pollen, dropping sweetly.

Sometimes poems come to me in pieces;
I place them in a junk drawer
until it cannot close anymore.

Then, methodically, I spread them out:
tiny little things, like baby teeth kept
and browning in a medicine bottle,
and listen to them rattle into song.

Cured

I.
I am afraid of that sea;
that sea that will divide
me from
        you; separate our
souls into bits of loss,
swallowed by serpentine mouths.
That I will smell olive oil,
and your name will become
water.

II.
A sore forms, deep,
acidic, and strong,
attaches to a heart wall;
        pumps.
I tell you, and you suck the venom
out clean as a snakebite
and leave a kiss behind—
cured.

Fried Eggs

I bought organic eggs—$3.99 + tax—
and meandered halfway down the aisle
(frozen hash browns, orange juice cans, butter),
before I remembered:
>*check the eggs.*

And so, I did; they were beautiful.

Speckled and tan, all twelve sat delicately
in their plastic cups, smooth as cold apple skin.
I placed them in the cart,
bagged them separately,
drove home slowly.

This morning
I rose somberly from bed, feeling strange and
dismembered, and cracked two of the holy
twelve into the oiled frying pan.
The yolks gravitated to the center,
the dog licked my heels, and I
broke out into poetry.

About the Author

Catherine Carson studied poetry at James Madison University but was writing long before that. Her love affair with poetry began at the age of fifteen and has never stopped. With heroes like Slyvia Plath, Joy Harjo, and Mary Oliver, Catherine writes confessional-style poetry in free verse. Her subjects include mental illness, womanhood, relationships and friendships, and the experiences of youth. After winning the JMU Creative Writing faculty's poetry award and being published in *Dreamers Creative Writing Magazine*, Catherine decided to pursue poetry as a profession, writing formally in workshops as well as in her spare time. She regards writing poetry as both a need and a want, and will continue to publish more work.

www.ingramcontent.com/pod-product-compliance
Lightning Source LLC
Chambersburg PA
CBHW020023050426
42450CB00005B/609